HAL•LEONARD

JAZZ PLAY-ALONG®

ok and CD for B♭, E♭, C and Bass Clef Instruments

volume 95

JAZZ at the Lounge

10 Cool Favorites

Arranged and Produced by
Mark Taylor

BOOK

CD

ISBN 978-1-4234-5910-1

HAL•LEONARD®
CORPORATION

7777 W. BLUEMOUND RD. P.O. BOX 13819 MILWAUKEE, WI 53213

Visit Hal Leonard Online at
www.halleonard.com

Jazz at the Lounge

Volume 95

Arranged and Produced by
Mark Taylor

Featured Players:

Graham Breedlove–Trumpet
Scott Silbert–Tenor Saxophone
Tony Nalker–Piano
Jim Roberts–Bass
Joe McCarthy–Drums

**Recorded at Bias Studios, Springfield, Virginia
Bob Dawson, Engineer**

HOW TO USE THE CD:

Each song has <u>two</u> tracks:

1) Split Track/Melody

Woodwind, Brass, Keyboard, and **Mallet Players** can use this track as a learning tool for melody style and inflection.

Bass Players can learn and perform with this track – remove the recorded bass track by turning down the volume on the LEFT channel.

Keyboard and **Guitar Players** can learn and perform with this track – remove the recorded piano part by turning down the volume on the RIGHT channel.

2) Full Stereo Track

Soloists or **Groups** can learn and perform with this accompaniment track with the RHYTHM SECTION only.

All My Tomorrows

CD
1 : SPLIT TRACK/MELODY
2 : FULL STEREO TRACK

C VERSION

WORDS BY SAMMY CAHN
MUSIC BY JAMES VAN HEUSEN

ALL THE WAY

WORDS BY SAMMY CAHN
MUSIC BY JAMES VAN HEUSEN

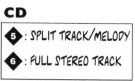

Beyond the Sea

BY ALBERT LASRY AND CHARLES TRENET
ENGLISH LYRICS BY JACK LAWRENCE

I LEFT MY HEART IN SAN FRANCISCO

CD
7 : SPLIT TRACK/MELODY
8 : FULL STEREO TRACK

WORDS BY DOUGLASS CROSS
MUSIC BY GEORGE CORY

C VERSION

L-O-V-E

CD
◆ 9 : SPLIT TRACK/MELODY
◆ 10 : FULL STEREO TRACK

C VERSION

WORDS AND MUSIC BY BERT KAEMPFERT
AND MILT GABLER

MONA LISA

WORDS AND MUSIC BY JAY LIVINGSTON
AND RAY EVANS

CD
- **13** : SPLIT TRACK/MELODY
- **14** : FULL STEREO TRACK

C VERSION

SWAY
(QUIEN SERÁ)

ENGLISH WORDS BY NORMAN GIMBEL
SPANISH WORDS AND MUSIC BY PABLO BELTRÁN RUIZ

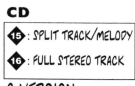

(LOVE IS)
THE TENDER TRAP

WORDS BY SAMMY CAHN
MUSIC BY JAMES VAN HEUSEN

C VERSION

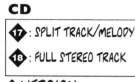

WHAT A WONDERFUL WORLD

WORDS AND MUSIC BY GEORGE DAVID WEISS
AND BOB THIELE

C VERSION

CD
19 : SPLIT TRACK/MELODY
20 : FULL STEREO TRACK

C VERSION

YOU'RE NOBODY 'TIL SOMEBODY LOVES YOU

WORDS AND MUSIC BY RUSS MORGAN, LARRY STOCK AND JAMES CAVANAUGH

ALL MY TOMORROWS

WORDS BY SAMMY CAHN
MUSIC BY JAMES VAN HEUSEN

CD
1 : SPLIT TRACK/MELODY
2 : FULL STEREO TRACK

Bb VERSION

CD

3 : SPLIT TRACK/MELODY
4 : FULL STEREO TRACK

Bb VERSION

All The Way

WORDS BY SAMMY CAHN
MUSIC BY JAMES VAN HEUSEN

Beyond the Sea

BY ALBERT LASRY AND CHARLES TRENET
ENGLISH LYRICS BY JACK LAWRENCE

29

I LEFT MY HEART IN SAN FRANCISCO

WORDS BY DOUGLASS CROSS
MUSIC BY GEORGE CORY

CD

7 : SPLIT TRACK/MELODY
8 : FULL STEREO TRACK

Bb VERSION

L-O-V-E

WORDS AND MUSIC BY BERT KAEMPFERT
AND MILT GABLER

MONA LISA

WORDS AND MUSIC BY JAY LIVINGSTON
AND RAY EVANS

CD
- **11**: SPLIT TRACK/MELODY
- **12**: FULL STEREO TRACK

Bb VERSION

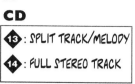

CD

13 : SPLIT TRACK/MELODY
14 : FULL STEREO TRACK

SWAY
(QUIEN SERÁ)

ENGLISH WORDS BY NORMAN GIMBEL
SPANISH WORDS AND MUSIC BY PABLO BELTRÁN RUIZ

Bb VERSION

CD

- ◆15: SPLIT TRACK/MELODY
- ◆16: FULL STEREO TRACK

(LOVE IS)
THE TENDER TRAP

WORDS BY SAMMY CAHN
MUSIC BY JAMES VAN HEUSEN

Bb VERSION

WHAT A WONDERFUL WORLD

WORDS AND MUSIC BY GEORGE DAVID WEISS
AND BOB THIELE

CD
17 : SPLIT TRACK/MELODY
18 : FULL STEREO TRACK

Bb VERSION

YOU'RE NOBODY 'TIL SOMEBODY LOVES YOU

Bb VERSION

WORDS AND MUSIC BY RUSS MORGAN,
LARRY STOCK AND JAMES CAVANAUGH

ALL MY TOMORROWS

WORDS BY SAMMY CAHN
MUSIC BY JAMES VAN HEUSEN

CD
1 : SPLIT TRACK/MELODY
2 : FULL STEREO TRACK

Eb VERSION

45

All The Way

WORDS BY SAMMY CAHN
MUSIC BY JAMES VAN HEUSEN

Eb VERSION

BEYOND THE SEA

BY ALBERT LASRY AND CHARLES TRENET
ENGLISH LYRICS BY JACK LAWRENCE

I LEFT MY HEART IN SAN FRANCISCO

WORDS BY DOUGLASS CROSS
MUSIC BY GEORGE CORY

Eb VERSION

L-O-V-E

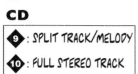

WORDS AND MUSIC BY BERT KAEMPFERT
AND MILT GABLER

Eb VERSION

MONA LISA

WORDS AND MUSIC BY JAY LIVINGSTON
AND RAY EVANS

Eb VERSION

CD

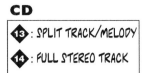

⟨13⟩ : SPLIT TRACK/MELODY
⟨14⟩ : FULL STEREO TRACK

Eb VERSION

SWAY
(QUIEN SERÁ)

ENGLISH WORDS BY NORMAN GIMBEL
SPANISH WORDS AND MUSIC BY PABLO BELTRÁN RUIZ

TO CODA ⊕

CD

15 : SPLIT TRACK/MELODY
16 : FULL STEREO TRACK

Eb VERSION

(LOVE IS)
THE TENDER TRAP

WORDS BY SAMMY CAHN
MUSIC BY JAMES VAN HEUSEN

WHAT A WONDERFUL WORLD

CD
17 : SPLIT TRACK/MELODY
18 : FULL STEREO TRACK

Eb VERSION

WORDS AND MUSIC BY GEORGE DAVID WEISS
AND BOB THIELE

You're Nobody 'Til Somebody Loves You

WORDS AND MUSIC BY RUSS MORGAN,
LARRY STOCK AND JAMES CAVANAUGH

Eb VERSION

ALL MY TOMORROWS

WORDS BY SAMMY CAHN
MUSIC BY JAMES VAN HEUSEN

CD
1 : SPLIT TRACK/MELODY
2 : FULL STEREO TRACK

C VERSION

MEDIUM SWING BALLAD

All The Way

WORDS BY SAMMY CAHN
MUSIC BY JAMES VAN HEUSEN

CD
◆3 : SPLIT TRACK/MELODY
◆4 : FULL STEREO TRACK

𝄢: C VERSION

Beyond the Sea

BY ALBERT LASRY AND CHARLES TRENET
ENGLISH LYRICS BY JACK LAWRENCE

I LEFT MY HEART IN SAN FRANCISCO

WORDS BY DOUGLASS CROSS
MUSIC BY GEORGE CORY

L-O-V-E

WORDS AND MUSIC BY BERT KAEMPFERT
AND MILT GABLER

CD

⏴11⏵: SPLIT TRACK/MELODY
⏴12⏵: FULL STEREO TRACK

𝄢 C VERSION

MONA LISA

WORDS AND MUSIC BY JAY LIVINGSTON
AND RAY EVANS

SLOW BOSSA

CD
- **13**: SPLIT TRACK/MELODY
- **14**: FULL STEREO TRACK

SWAY
(QUIEN SERÁ)

ENGLISH WORDS BY NORMAN GIMBEL
SPANISH WORDS AND MUSIC BY PABLO BELTRÁN RUIZ

𝄢: C VERSION

CD

15 : SPLIT TRACK/MELODY
16 : FULL STEREO TRACK

🎜: C VERSION

(LOVE IS)
THE TENDER TRAP

WORDS BY SAMMY CAHN
MUSIC BY JAMES VAN HEUSEN

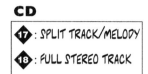

WHAT A WONDERFUL WORLD

WORDS AND MUSIC BY GEORGE DAVID WEISS
AND BOB THIELE

CD
19 : SPLIT TRACK/MELODY
20 : FULL STEREO TRACK

YOU'RE NOBODY 'TIL SOMEBODY LOVES YOU

WORDS AND MUSIC BY RUSS MORGAN, LARRY STOCK AND JAMES CAVANAUGH

🎼: C VERSION

For use with all B-flat, E-flat, Bass Clef and C instruments, the Jazz Play-Along® Series is the ultimate learning tool for all jazz musicians. With musician-friendly lead sheets, melody cues, and other split-track audio choices included, these first-of-a-kind packages help you master improvisation while playing some of the greatest tunes of all time. FOR STUDY, each tune includes a split track with: melody cue with proper style and inflection • professional rhythm tracks • choruses for soloing • removable bass part • removable piano part. FOR PERFORMANCE, each tune also has: an additional full stereo accompaniment track (no melody) • additional choruses for soloing.

1A. MAIDEN VOYAGE/ALL BLUES
00843158 .... $15.99

1. DUKE ELLINGTON
00841644 .... $16.99

2. MILES DAVIS
00841645 .... $16.99

3. THE BLUES
00841646 .... $16.99

4. JAZZ BALLADS
00841691 .... $16.99

5. BEST OF BEBOP
00841689 .... $16.99

6. JAZZ CLASSICS WITH EASY CHANGES
00841690 .... $16.99

7. ESSENTIAL JAZZ STANDARDS
00843000 .... $16.99

8. ANTONIO CARLOS JOBIM AND THE ART OF THE BOSSA NOVA
00843001 .... $16.99

9. DIZZY GILLESPIE
00843002 .... $16.99

10. DISNEY CLASSICS
00843003 .... $16.99

12. ESSENTIAL JAZZ CLASSICS
00843005 .... $16.99

13. JOHN COLTRANE
00843006 .... $16.99

14. IRVING BERLIN
00843007 .... $16.99

15. RODGERS & HAMMERSTEIN
00843008 .... $16.99

16. COLE PORTER
00843009 .... $16.99

17. COUNT BASIE
00843010 .... $16.99

18. HAROLD ARLEN
00843011 .... $16.99

20. CHRISTMAS CAROLS
00843080 .... $16.99

21. RODGERS AND HART CLASSICS
00843014 .... $16.99

22. WAYNE SHORTER
00843015 .... $16.99

23. LATIN JAZZ
00843016 .... $16.99

24. EARLY JAZZ STANDARDS
00843017 .... $16.99

25. CHRISTMAS JAZZ
00843018 .... $16.99

26. CHARLIE PARKER
00843019 .... $16.99

27. GREAT JAZZ STANDARDS
00843020 .... $16.99

28. BIG BAND ERA
00843021 .... $16.99

29. LENNON AND MCCARTNEY
00843022 .... $16.99

30. BLUES' BEST
00843023 .... $16.99

31. JAZZ IN THREE
00843024 .... $16.99

32. BEST OF SWING
00843025 .... $17.99

33. SONNY ROLLINS
00843029 .... $16.99

34. ALL TIME STANDARDS
00843030 .... $16.99

35. BLUESY JAZZ
00843031 .... $16.99

36. HORACE SILVER
00843032 .... $16.99

37. BILL EVANS
00843033 .... $16.99

38. YULETIDE JAZZ
00843034 .... $16.99

39. "ALL THE THINGS YOU ARE" & MORE JEROME KERN SONGS
00843035 .... $16.99

40. BOSSA NOVA
00843036 .... $16.99

41. CLASSIC DUKE ELLINGTON
00843037 .... $16.99

42. GERRY MULLIGAN FAVORITES
00843038 .... $16.99

43. GERRY MULLIGAN CLASSICS
00843039 .... $16.99

45. GEORGE GERSHWIN
00103643 .... $24.99

47. CLASSIC JAZZ BALLADS
00843043 .... $16.99

48. BEBOP CLASSICS
00843044 .... $16.99

49. MILES DAVIS STANDARDS
00843045 .... $16.99

52. STEVIE WONDER
00843048 .... $16.99

53. RHYTHM CHANGES
00843049 .... $16.99

55. BENNY GOLSON
00843052 .... $16.99

56. "GEORGIA ON MY MIND" & OTHER SONGS BY HOAGY CARMICHAEL
00843056 .... $16.99

57. VINCE GUARALDI
00843057 .... $16.99

58. MORE LENNON AND MCCARTNEY
00843059 .... $16.99

59. SOUL JAZZ
00843060 .... $16.99

60. DEXTER GORDON
00843061 .... $16.99

61. MONGO SANTAMARIA
00843062 .... $16.99

62. JAZZ-ROCK FUSION
00843063 .... $16.99

63. CLASSICAL JAZZ
00843064 .... $16.99

64. TV TUNES
00843065 .... $16.99

65. SMOOTH JAZZ
00843066 .... $16.99

66. A CHARLIE BROWN CHRISTMAS
00843067 .... $16.99

67. CHICK COREA
00843068 .... $16.99

68. CHARLES MINGUS
00843069 .... $16.99

71. COLE PORTER CLASSICS
00843073 .... $16.99

72. CLASSIC JAZZ BALLADS
00843074 .... $16.99

73. JAZZ/BLUES
00843075 .... $16.99

74. BEST JAZZ CLASSICS
00843076 .... $16.99

75. PAUL DESMOND
00843077 .... $16.99

78. STEELY DAN
00843070 .... $16.99

79. MILES DAVIS CLASSICS
00843081 .... $16.99

80. JIMI HENDRIX
00843083 .... $16.99

83. ANDREW LLOYD WEBBER
00843104 .... $16.99

84. BOSSA NOVA CLASSICS
00843105 .... $16.99

85. MOTOWN HITS
00843109 .... $16.99

86. BENNY GOODMAN
00843110 .... $16.99

87. DIXIELAND
00843111 .... $16.99

90. **THELONIOUS MONK CLASSICS**
00841262 ....$16.99

91. **THELONIOUS MONK FAVORITES**
00841263 ....$16.99

92. **LEONARD BERNSTEIN**
00450134 ....$16.99

93. **DISNEY FAVORITES**
00843142 ....$16.99

94. **RAY**
00843143 ....$16.99

95. **JAZZ AT THE LOUNGE**
00843144 ....$16.99

96. **LATIN JAZZ STANDARDS**
00843145 ....$16.99

97. **MAYBE I'M AMAZED***
00843148 ....$16.99

98. **DAVE FRISHBERG**
00843149 ....$16.99

99. **SWINGING STANDARDS**
00843150 ....$16.99

100. **LOUIS ARMSTRONG**
00740423 ....$16.99

101. **BUD POWELL**
00843152 ....$16.99

102. **JAZZ POP**
00843153 ....$16.99

103. **ON GREEN DOLPHIN STREET
& OTHER JAZZ CLASSICS**
00843154 ....$16.99

104. **ELTON JOHN**
00843155 ....$16.99

105. **SOULFUL JAZZ**
00843151 ....$16.99

106. **SLO' JAZZ**
00843117 ....$16.99

107. **MOTOWN CLASSICS**
00843116 ....$16.99

108. **JAZZ WALTZ**
00843159 ....$16.99

109. **OSCAR PETERSON**
00843160 ....$16.99

110. **JUST STANDARDS**
00843161 ....$16.99

111. **COOL CHRISTMAS**
00843162 ....$16.99

112. **PAQUITO D'RIVERA – LATIN JAZZ***
48020662 ....$16.99

113. **PAQUITO D'RIVERA – BRAZILIAN JAZZ***
48020663 ....$19.99

114. **MODERN JAZZ QUARTET FAVORITES**
00843163 ....$16.99

115. **THE SOUND OF MUSIC**
00843164 ....$16.99

116. **JACO PASTORIUS**
00843165 ....$16.99

117. **ANTONIO CARLOS JOBIM – MORE HITS**
00843166 ....$16.99

118. **BIG JAZZ STANDARDS COLLECTION**
00843167 ....$27.50

119. **JELLY ROLL MORTON**
00843168 ....$16.99

120. **J.S. BACH**
00843169 ....$16.99

121. **DJANGO REINHARDT**
00843170 ....$16.99

122. **PAUL SIMON**
00843182 ....$16.99

123. **BACHARACH & DAVID**
00843185 ....$16.99

124. **JAZZ-ROCK HORN HITS**
00843186 ....$16.99

125. **SAMMY NESTICO**
00843187 ....$16.99

126. **COUNT BASIE CLASSICS**
00843157 ....$16.99

127. **CHUCK MANGIONE**
00843188 ....$16.99

128. **VOCAL STANDARDS (LOW VOICE)**
00843189 ....$16.99

129. **VOCAL STANDARDS (HIGH VOICE)**
00843190 ....$16.99

130. **VOCAL JAZZ (LOW VOICE)**
00843191 ....$16.99

131. **VOCAL JAZZ (HIGH VOICE)**
00843192 ....$16.99

132. **STAN GETZ ESSENTIALS**
00843193 ....$16.99

133. **STAN GETZ FAVORITES**
00843194 ....$16.99

134. **NURSERY RHYMES***
00843196 ....$17.99

135. **JEFF BECK**
00843197 ....$16.99

136. **NAT ADDERLEY**
00843198 ....$16.99

137. **WES MONTGOMERY**
00843199 ....$16.99

138. **FREDDIE HUBBARD**
00843200 ....$16.99

139. **JULIAN "CANNONBALL" ADDERLEY**
00843201 ....$16.99

140. **JOE ZAWINUL**
00843202 ....$16.99

141. **BILL EVANS STANDARDS**
00843156 ....$16.99

142. **CHARLIE PARKER GEMS**
00843222 ....$16.99

143. **JUST THE BLUES**
00843223 ....$16.99

144. **LEE MORGAN**
00843229 ....$16.99

145. **COUNTRY STANDARDS**
00843230 ....$16.99

146. **RAMSEY LEWIS**
00843231 ....$16.99

147. **SAMBA**
00843232 ....$16.99

148. **JOHN COLTRANE FAVORITES**
00843233 ....$16.99

149. **JOHN COLTRANE – GIANT STEPS**
00843234 ....$16.99

150. **JAZZ IMPROV BASICS**
00843195 ....$19.99

151. **MODERN JAZZ QUARTET CLASSICS**
00843209 ....$16.99

152. **J.J. JOHNSON**
00843210 ....$16.99

153. **KENNY GARRETT**
00843212 ....$16.99

154. **HENRY MANCINI**
00843213 ....$16.99

155. **SMOOTH JAZZ CLASSICS**
00843215 ....$16.99

156. **THELONIOUS MONK – EARLY GEMS**
00843216 ....$16.99

157. **HYMNS**
00843217 ....$16.99

158. **JAZZ COVERS ROCK**
00843219 ....$16.99

159. **MOZART**
00843220 ....$16.99

160. **GEORGE SHEARING**
14041531 ....$16.99

161. **DAVE BRUBECK**
14041556 ....$16.99

162. **BIG CHRISTMAS COLLECTION**
00843221 ....$24.99

163. **JOHN COLTRANE STANDARDS**
00843235 ....$16.99

164. **HERB ALPERT**
14041775 ....$16.99

165. **GEORGE BENSON**
00843240 ....$16.99

166. **ORNETTE COLEMAN**
00843241 ....$16.99

167. **JOHNNY MANDEL**
00103642 ....$16.99

168. **TADD DAMERON**
00103663 ....$16.99

169. **BEST JAZZ STANDARDS**
00109249 ....$19.99

170. **ULTIMATE JAZZ STANDARDS**
00109250 ....$19.99

171. **RADIOHEAD**
00109305 ....$16.99

172. **POP STANDARDS**
00111669 ....$16.99

174. **TIN PAN ALLEY**
00119125 ....$16.99

175. **TANGO**
00119836 ....$16.99

176. **JOHNNY MERCER**
00119838 ....$16.99

177. **THE II-V-I PROGRESSION**
00843239 ....$19.99

178. **JAZZ/FUNK**
00121902 ....$16.99

179. **MODAL JAZZ**
00122273 ....$16.99

180. **MICHAEL JACKSON**
00122327 ....$17.99

181. **BILLY JOEL**
00122329 ....$16.99

182. **"RHAPSODY IN BLUE" & 7 OTHER
CLASSICAL-BASED JAZZ PIECES**
00116847 ....$16.99

183. **SONDHEIM**
00126253 ....$16.99

184. **JIMMY SMITH**
00126943 ....$16.99

185. **JAZZ FUSION**
00127558 ....$16.99

186. **JOE PASS**
00128391 ....$16.99

187. **CHRISTMAS FAVORITES**
00128393 ....$16.99

188. **PIAZZOLLA – 10 FAVORITE TUNES**
48023253 ....$16.99

189. **JOHN LENNON**
00138678 ....$16.99

0418

*These do not include split tracks.

A R T I S T
TRANSCRIPTIONS®

Artist Transcriptions are authentic, note-for-note transcriptions of today's hottest artists in jazz, pop and rock. These outstanding, accurate arrangements are in an easy-to-read format which includes all essential lines. **Artist Transcriptions** can be used to perform, sequence or for reference.

CLARINET

00672423	Buddy De Franco Collection	$19.95

FLUTE

00672379	Eric Dolphy Collection	$19.95
00672582	The Very Best of James Galway	$16.99
00672372	James Moody Collection – Sax and Flute	$19.95

GUITAR & BASS

00660113	The Guitar Style of George Benson	$16.99
00699072	Guitar Book of Pierre Bensusan	$29.95
00672331	Ron Carter – Acoustic Bass	$19.99
00672573	Ray Brown – Legendary Jazz Bassist	$19.99
00672307	Stanley Clarke Collection	$19.99
00660115	Al Di Meola – Friday Night in San Francisco	$16.99
00604043	Al Di Meola – Music, Words, Pictures	$14.95
00672574	Al Di Meola – Pursuit of Radical Rhapsody	$22.99
00125617	Best of Herb Ellis	$19.99
00673245	Jazz Style of Tal Farlow	$19.99
00699306	Jim Hall – Exploring Jazz Guitar	$19.99
00604049	Allan Holdsworth – Reaching for the Uncommon Chord	$17.99
00699215	Leo Kottke – Eight Songs	$17.99
00672353	Joe Pass Collection	$19.99
00673216	John Patitucci	$17.99
00027083	Django Reinhardt Anthology	$16.99
00672374	Johnny Smith Guitar Solos	$19.99

PIANO & KEYBOARD

00672338	Monty Alexander Collection	$19.95
00672487	Monty Alexander Plays Standards	$19.95
00672520	Count Basie Collection	$19.95
00192307	Bebop Piano Legends	$19.99
00113680	Blues Piano Legends	$19.99
00278003	A Charlie Brown Christmas	$17.99
00672439	Cyrus Chestnut Collection	$19.95
00672300	Chick Corea – Paint the World	$16.99
14037739	Storyville Presents Duke Ellington	$19.99
00146105	Bill Evans – Alone	$17.99
00672537	Bill Evans at Town Hall	$19.99
00672548	The Mastery of Bill Evans	$16.99
00672425	Bill Evans – Piano Interpretations	$22.99
00672365	Bill Evans – Piano Standards	$19.99
00121885	Bill Evans – Time Remembered	$19.99
00672510	Bill Evans Trio – Vol. 1: 1959-1961	$24.95
00672511	Bill Evans Trio – Vol. 2: 1962-1965	$24.99
00672512	Bill Evans Trio – Vol. 3: 1968-1974	$24.99
00672513	Bill Evans Trio – Vol. 4: 1979-1980	$24.95
00672381	Tommy Flanagan Collection	$24.99
00193332	Erroll Garner – Concert by the Sea	$19.99
00672492	Benny Goodman Collection	$16.95
00672486	Vince Guaraldi Collection	$19.99
00672419	Herbie Hancock Collection	$19.95
00672438	Hampton Hawes	$19.95
14037738	Storyville Presents Earl Hines	$19.99

00672322	Ahmad Jamal Collection	$24.99
00255671	Jazz Piano Masterpieces	$19.99
00124367	Jazz Piano Masters Play Rodgers & Hammerstein	$19.99
00672564	Best of Jeff Lorber	$17.99
00672476	Brad Mehldau Collection	$19.99
00672388	Best of Thelonious Monk	$19.95
00672389	Thelonious Monk Collection	$22.99
00672390	Thelonious Monk Plays Jazz Standards – Volume 1	$19.99
00672391	Thelonious Monk Plays Jazz Standards – Volume 2	$19.95
00672433	Jelly Roll Morton – The Piano Rolls	$16.99
00672553	Charlie Parker for Piano	$19.95
00672542	Oscar Peterson – Jazz Piano Solos	$17.99
00672562	Oscar Peterson – A Jazz Portrait of Frank Sinatra	$19.95
00264094	Oscar Peterson – Night Train	$19.99
00672544	Oscar Peterson – Originals	$10.99
00672532	Oscar Peterson – Plays Broadway	$19.95
00672531	Oscar Peterson – Plays Duke Ellington	$24.99
00672563	Oscar Peterson – A Royal Wedding Suite	$19.99
00672569	Oscar Peterson – Tracks	$19.99
00672533	Oscar Peterson – Trios	$24.95
00672543	Oscar Peterson Trio – Canadiana Suite	$12.99
00672534	Very Best of Oscar Peterson	$22.95
00672371	Bud Powell Classics	$19.99
00672376	Bud Powell Collection	$19.95
00672507	Gonzalo Rubalcaba Collection	$19.95
00672303	Horace Silver Collection	$22.99
00672316	Art Tatum Collection	$24.99
00672355	Art Tatum Solo Book	$19.95
00673215	McCoy Tyner	$19.99
00672321	Cedar Walton Collection	$19.95
00672519	Kenny Werner Collection	$19.95
00672434	Teddy Wilson Collection	$19.95

SAXOPHONE

00672566	The Mindi Abair Collection	$14.99
00673244	Julian "Cannonball" Adderley Collection	$19.95
00673237	Michael Brecker	$19.95
00672429	Michael Brecker Collection	$22.99
00672315	Benny Carter Plays Standards	$22.95
00672394	James Carter Collection	$19.95
00672349	John Coltrane Plays Giant Steps	$19.95
00672529	John Coltrane – Giant Steps	$17.99
00672494	John Coltrane – A Love Supreme	$15.99
00307393	John Coltrane – Omnibook: C Instruments	$24.99
00307391	John Coltrane – Omnibook: B-flat Instruments	$27.99
00307392	John Coltrane – Omnibook: E-flat Instruments	$29.99
00307394	John Coltrane – Omnibook: Bass Clef Instruments	$24.99

00672493	John Coltrane Plays "Coltrane Changes"	$19.95
00672453	John Coltrane Plays Standards	$22.99
00673233	John Coltrane Solos	$22.95
00672328	Paul Desmond Collection	$19.95
00672379	Eric Dolphy Collection	$19.95
00672530	Kenny Garrett Collection	$19.95
00699375	Stan Getz	$19.99
00672377	Stan Getz – Bossa Novas	$22.99
00672375	Stan Getz – Standards	$19.99
00673254	Great Tenor Sax Solos	$18.99
00672523	Coleman Hawkins Collection	$19.99
00673252	Joe Henderson – Selections from "Lush Life" & "So Near So Far"	$19.95
00673239	Best of Kenny G	$19.95
00673229	Kenny G – Breathless	$19.95
00672462	Kenny G – Classics in the Key of G	$19.95
00672485	Kenny G – Faith: A Holiday Album	$15.99
00672373	Kenny G – The Moment	$19.95
00672498	Jackie McLean Collection	$19.95
00672372	James Moody Collection – Sax and Flute	$19.95
00672416	Frank Morgan Collection	$19.95
00672539	Gerry Mulligan Collection	$19.95
00672352	Charlie Parker Collection	$19.95
00672561	Best of Sonny Rollins	$19.95
00102751	Sonny Rollins with the Modern Jazz Quartet	$17.99
00675000	David Sanborn Collection	$19.99
00672491	New Best of Wayne Shorter	$22.99
00672550	The Sonny Stitt Collection	$19.95
00672524	Lester Young Collection	$19.99

TROMBONE

00672332	J.J. Johnson Collection	$19.99
00672489	Steve Turré Collection	$19.99

TRUMPET

00672557	Herb Alpert Collection	$17.99
00672480	Louis Armstrong Collection	$19.99
00672481	Louis Armstrong Plays Standards	$19.99
00672435	Chet Baker Collection	$19.99
00672556	Best of Chris Botti	$19.99
00672448	Miles Davis – Originals, Vol. 1	$19.95
00672451	Miles Davis – Originals, Vol. 2	$19.99
00672450	Miles Davis – Standards, Vol. 1	$19.99
00672449	Miles Davis – Standards, Vol. 2	$19.95
00672479	Dizzy Gillespie Collection	$19.95
00673214	Freddie Hubbard	$19.99
00672382	Tom Harrell – Jazz Trumpet	$19.95
00672363	Jazz Trumpet Solos	$9.95
00672506	Chuck Mangione Collection	$19.95
00672525	Arturo Sandoval – Trumpet Evolution	$19.99

HAL•LEONARD®
7777 W. BLUEMOUND RD. P.O. BOX 13819 MILWAUKEE, WI 53213

Visit our web site for a complete listing of our titles with songlists at
www.halleonard.com

0619

Jazz Instruction & Improvisation

BOOKS FOR ALL INSTRUMENTS FROM HAL LEONARD

AN APPROACH TO JAZZ IMPROVISATION
by Dave Pozzi
Musicians Institute Press
Explore the styles of Charlie Parker, Sonny Rollins, Bud Powell and others with this comprehensive guide to jazz improvisation. Covers: scale choices • chord analysis • phrasing • melodies • harmonic progressions • more.
00695135 Book/CD Pack........................$17.95

THE ART OF MODULATING
FOR PIANISTS AND JAZZ MUSICIANS
by Carlos Salzedo &
Lucile Lawrence
Schirmer
The Art of Modulating is a treatise originally intended for the harp, but this edition has been edited for use by intermediate keyboardists and other musicians who have an understanding of basic music theory. In its pages you will find: table of intervals; modulation rules; modulation formulas; examples of modulation; extensions and cadences; ten fragments of dances; five characteristic pieces; and more.
50490581 ....$19.99

BUILDING A JAZZ VOCABULARY
By Mike Steinel
A valuable resource for learning the basics of jazz from Mike Steinel of the University of North Texas. It covers: the basics of jazz • how to build effective solos • a comprehensive practice routine • and a jazz vocabulary of the masters.
00849911 ....$19.99

THE CYCLE OF FIFTHS
by Emile and Laura De Cosmo
This essential instruction book provides more than 450 exercises, including hundreds of melodic and rhythmic ideas. The book is designed to help improvisors master the cycle of fifths, one of the primary progressions in music. Guaranteed to refine technique, enhance improvisational fluency, and improve sight-reading!
00311114 ....$16.99

THE DIATONIC CYCLE
by Emile and Laura De Cosmo
Renowned jazz educators Emile and Laura De Cosmo provide more than 300 exercises to help improvisors tackle one of music's most common progressions: the diatonic cycle. This book is guaranteed to refine technique, enhance improvisational fluency, and improve sight-reading!
00311115 ....$16.95

EAR TRAINING
by Keith Wyatt,
Carl Schroeder and Joe Elliott
Musicians Institute Press
Covers: basic pitch matching • singing major and minor scales • identifying intervals • transcribing melodies and rhythm • identifying chords and progressions • seventh chords and the blues • modal interchange, chromaticism, modulation • and more.
00695198 Book/Online Audio $24.99

EXERCISES AND ETUDES FOR THE JAZZ INSTRUMENTALIST
by J.J. Johnson
Designed as study material and playable by any instrument, these pieces run the gamut of the jazz experience, featuring common and uncommon time signatures and keys, and styles from ballads to funk. They are progressively graded so that both beginners and professionals will be challenged by the demands of this wonderful music.
00842018 Bass Clef Edition $19.99
00842042 Treble Clef Edition $16.95

JAZZOLOGY
THE ENCYCLOPEDIA OF JAZZ THEORY FOR ALL MUSICIANS
by Robert Rawlins and
Nor Eddine Bahha
This comprehensive resource covers a variety of jazz topics, for beginners and pros of any instrument. The book serves as an encyclopedia for reference, a thorough methodology for the student, and a workbook for the classroom.
00311167 ....$19.99

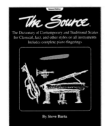

JAZZ THEORY RESOURCES
by Bert Ligon
Houston Publishing, Inc.
This is a jazz theory text in two volumes. **Volume 1 includes**: review of basic theory • rhythm in jazz performance • triadic generalization • diatonic harmonic progressions and analysis • substitutions and turnarounds • and more. **Volume 2 includes**: modes and modal frameworks • quartal harmony • extended tertian structures and triadic superimposition • pentatonic applications • coloring "outside" the lines and beyond • and more.
00030458 Volume 1 ....$39.99
00030459 Volume 2 ....$32.99

JOY OF IMPROV
by Dave Frank
and John Amaral
This book/audio course on improvisation for all instruments and all styles will help players develop monster musical skills! Book One imparts a solid basis in technique, rhythm, chord theory, ear training and improv concepts. **Book Two** explores more advanced chord voicings, chord arranging techniques and more challenging blues and melodic lines. The audio can be used as a listening and play-along tool.
00220005 Book 1 – Book/Online Audio................$27.99
00220006 Book 2 – Book/Online Audio................$26.99

THE PATH TO JAZZ IMPROVISATION
by Emile and Laura De Cosmo
This fascinating jazz instruction book offers an innovative, scholarly approach to the art of improvisation. It includes in-depth analysis and lessons about: cycle of fifths • diatonic cycle • overtone series • pentatonic scale • harmonic and melodic minor scale • polytonal order of keys • blues and bebop scales • modes • and more.
00310904 ....$19.99

THE SOURCE
THE DICTIONARY OF CONTEMPORARY AND TRADITIONAL SCALES
by Steve Barta
This book serves as an informative guide for people who are looking for good, solid information regarding scales, chords, and how they work together. It provides right and left hand fingerings for scales, chords, and complete inversions. Includes over 20 different scales, each written in all 12 keys.
00240885 ....$19.99

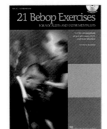

21 BEBOP EXERCISES
by Steve Rawlins
This book/CD pack is both a warm-up collection and a manual for bebop phrasing. Its tasty and sophisticated exercises will help you develop your proficiency with jazz interpretation. It concentrates on practice in all twelve keys – moving higher by half-step – to help develop dexterity and range. The companion CD includes all of the exercises in 12 keys.
00315341 Book/CD Pack....................................$17.95

HAL•LEONARD®
7777 W. BLUEMOUND RD. P.O. BOX 13819 MILWAUKEE, WI 53213

Visit Hal Leonard online at
www.halleonard.com

Prices, contents & availability subject to change without notice.

0419
068

The Best-Selling Jazz Book of All Time Is Now Legal!

The Real Books are the most popular jazz books of all time. Since the 1970s, musicians have trusted these volumes to get them through every gig, night after night. The problem is that the books were illegally produced and distributed, without any regard to copyright law, or royalties paid to the composers who created these musical masterpieces.

Hal Leonard is very proud to present the first legitimate and legal editions of these books ever produced. You won't even notice the difference, other than all the notorious errors being fixed: the covers and typeface look the same, the song lists are nearly identical, and the price for our edition is even cheaper than the originals!

VOLUME 1

00240221	C Edition	$39.99
00240224	B♭ Edition	$39.99
00240225	E♭ Edition	$39.99
00240226	Bass Clef Edition	$39.99
00286389	F Edition	$39.99
00240292	C Edition 6 x 9	$35.00
00240339	B♭ Edition 6 x 9	$35.00
00147792	Bass Clef Edition 6 x 9	$35.00
00451087	C Edition on CD-ROM	$29.99
00200984	Online Backing Tracks: Selections	$45.00
00110604	Book/USB Flash Drive Backing Tracks Pack	$79.99
00110599	USB Flash Drive Only	$50.00

VOLUME 2

00240222	C Edition	$39.99
00240227	B♭ Edition	$39.99
00240228	E♭ Edition	$39.99
00240229	Bass Clef Edition	$39.99
00240293	C Edition 6 x 9	$35.00
00125900	B♭ Edition 6 x 9	$35.00
00451088	C Edition on CD-ROM	$30.99
00125900	The Real Book – Mini Edition	$35.00
00204126	Backing Tracks on USB Flash Drive	$50.00
00204131	C Edition – USB Flash Drive Pack	$79.99

VOLUME 3

00240233	C Edition	$39.99
00240284	B♭ Edition	$39.99
00240285	E♭ Edition	$39.99
00240286	Bass Clef Edition	$39.99
00240338	C Edition 6 x 9	$35.00
00451089	C Edition on CD-ROM	$29.99

VOLUME 4

00240296	C Edition	$39.99
00103348	B♭ Edition	$39.99
00103349	E♭ Edition	$39.99
00103350	Bass Clef Edition	$39.99

VOLUME 5

00240349	C Edition	$39.99
00175278	B♭ Edition	$39.99
00175279	E♭ Edition	$39.99

VOLUME 6

00240534	C Edition	$39.99
00223637	E♭ Edition	$39.99

Also available:

00151290	The Real Book – Enhanced Chords	$29.99
00282973	The Reharmonized Real Book	$39.99

Complete song lists online at www.halleonard.com

Prices, content, and availability subject to change without notice.